The Beatles Landed
Laughing in New York

for my friends Gary, John and Roger
who share a passion for music
and for The Beatles
who changed everything

and as always
for Cathy and Mr. Two Boys

The Beatles Landed Laughing in New York

John B. Lee

Black Moss Press

©Copyright John B. Lee, 1995

Published by Black Moss Press
at 2450 Byng Road, Windsor, Ontario, N8W 3E8.
Black Moss Press books are distributed by Firefly Books Ltd.,
250 Sparks Avenue, Willowdale, Ontario, M2H 2S4.
All orders should be directed there.

Financial assistance toward publication of this book has been provided
by the The Canada Council and The Ontario Arts Council.

Cover design by Richard Withey

Canadian Cataloguing and Publication Data
Lee, John B., 1951—
The Beatles landed laughing in New York : poems
ISBN 0-88753-265-9

1. Title.
Ps8573.E348B43 1995   C911' .54   C95-900511-0
Pr919189.3.L39B43   1995

*poems from this collection have appeared in Arc, The Broadway, Prairie Fire, Word Up (an
anthology of poets appearing in Much Music's "Word Up" video series), "Word Up" (Much
Music's poetry video series) and a CD produced by Virgin Records based on the "Word Up"
poetry videos. "Cartesian TV" was published as a T-shirt poem by Flying Camel Press.

Contents

"... earl I ask from anybottly
that I grape me daily work
cronching our batter
My own bassoon."

from *Bernice's Sheep*
by John Lennon

You Are Snowmobiling, It is Midnight

i

You are snowmobiling, it is midnight.
The world is dirty white
in every direction.
You understand the icons of winter
with the purity of bathroom art.
The engine is ronronating
in love with the field.
Your headlight illuminates the coming of angels.
The dogwood whippets
snap around your skis.
The moon is smothered.
The farmer's brush pile
is hissing beneath the noise
like tea tossed in a fire.
Then you strike the fence
decolled, cut into sections
your body like a diagram
on a butcher's wall
or, you jump the ditch
hump a mogul, take a crooked furrow wrong
your tossed shape snapping a rotten branch
falling on its own weight
or, the ice gives way
like glass hit by a hammer
and you drop
dragged down by heavy engines
your arms thrashing
on the giving edge
engulfed in liquid darkness.

ii

(this is the moment
watching Robert Kennedy's eyes
lose the light
in the hotel kitchen.
                the moment
J.F.K.'s skull spores over the trunk
of the limousine.
                the moment
Lee Harvey Oswald
is gut shot in the basement
of a Dallas jail.
You see his sudden sharp wince of pain
and the rush of private confusion.
                the moment
the Buddhist monk douses
with gasoline, ignites his body
so he burns like a rag torch.
                the moment
the V.C. prisoner
takes the bullet in his brain
a political injection
his head jumps and he flops sideways
like a meat-packer's goat.

iii

You are skating.
It is a January afternoon.
The snow on the rim of the pond
is silting like lemonade sugar
where the dog has marked his longing.
You are
a gliding kite
that catches the wind without strings
in an important blue sky.

Then with one stride it all gives
and you go down
with a shocked step
waist deep
your skates cut into the mud
like knives into cake not quite cooked
and behind you
your wife shunts one leg into the water
like the shutting of a telescope.
And during the cold half mile walk to the house
your pants frosting stiff
cut around your legs like wimpled tin.
You remember the night
you trekked back
to where the old dog
was trapped in the hole
his haunches dipped in refreezing shards
where he whimpered and worried hurt
in the broken ice like a thief who'd jumped
half way through a door.

iv

(there's the famous moment
in the photograph of war
when the children strip themselves
of their chemical clothing
their flesh hot with napalm
the grief, the fear, the anguish
in their faces
so real
those of us with hearts
turn away and weep) our tears exploding
like tiny water balms as they hit the floor.

v

This is
the moment the marionettes of memory
go still
frozen in a tangle of strings
indifferent to the desires of art
feeling nothing
but the absolute inertia
felt on the verge of discovery.

When Doris Day Was in My Living Room

Remember the fifties
when Doris Day
was everybody's bread-and-butter blonde
and though she walked
like the bump of oranges
rolling away
from the gravity of the bowl
yet you knew
there was something in the hint
of movie darkness
called desire in women
something like fruit laid open
on the orchard grass
something
like the crease in apricots
where you might place your thumbs
something like winding
the stem of apples
to decode the alphabet of love
something like the hum
of flowers, occupied.
And she, setting one foot naked
on the floor beside the bed
sought in the midst of empty shoes
a proof of purity
a charm against the loss of light.

The Night The Beatles Sang into a Wall of Screams

Ed Sullivan
patron saint of circus bears
tuxedo magicians, lounge acts, and spinners of plates
owned Sunday night in Topo Gigiofied America
and the secular church of the cathode tube
where cocktail comics
and dancers hopping the clack of swords
surrounded the little man
with his neckless head
sinking into his ill-suited shoulders
and he brought us the Shakespearean parodies of Wayne and
Shuster
and he brought us Mitsy Gaynor, Frank Sinatra,
and the calculated cool of Dean Martin
with his smoking hand
so sleepy children rolled on rugs
and wished away Laurence Welk
Mitch Miller, Don Messer, Tommy Hunter
and all the other pale hungers of their parents
dull television lives
but then there was the night
in the moth-gray landscape
of late South-western Ontario winter
the night the Beatles sang
into a wall of screams
and into the faint farm smells
of our living room
with the straw still in my uncle's socks
and my mother
knitting nearby like a drummer with sticks
and no kit
and the low-down wool scent
of the braided brown oval rug
where I lay
half-bored and just a little conscious
before they took the stage.

ii

That ended for me
the politics of childhood
and girls came clear
as if I'd looked through water
at them til then
and I wanted words for that
and I wanted
to sing
suddenly and alone
til the cows came curious
to the fence
and I sat and wrote
and played the broomstick box
in my tiny room
and I strummed the broom
behind my grandfather's house
and followed the sound
across the hills
like the joy of birds
and I watched the dog
who looked at the radio
and thought, he knows it too
and even in summer
when he rattles his ears
to startle the flies
like Ringo Starr shaking his hair
it will still be there
—this change in things the music has made
this different colour in everything.

And Allen Ginsberg Danced

When American poet Allen Ginsberg
first heard the Beatles
he got up
like a Greek bridegroom and danced
the poems tumbling from his pockets
for a drunkard's paper change
and he danced
to weather and wind in the grassy hills
and he danced
of trapped water
where quiet horses drink
and he danced to the moon
in a mirror
as if all day his wild bald head
had been waiting
for Salome's signal
and he'd carried it in
on the platter of his shoulders
his black glasses
slipping down his nose
giving the world its vague ellipsis
and he danced
as if his careless body
were bitten by flies, stung by bees, struck by grass hoppers
singing his shirt from his ribs
and he danced
for all the ruined generations
and fallen kings
and he danced
as a wise old wolf
with a trap on his paw
who knows he still has three good legs left
to run the game.

And so they say, he never danced before
and I remember myself
awkward in the arms of my mother
with Guy Lumbardo on the box
while she was guiding me in the parlour
as if I'd spill at any moment
as if I were a bag of oranges chocked too full
the top ones tumbling out like bad juggling
and I remember myself years later
at my own wedding
with my sweet old Grandmother Busteed
dancing to the Stones—"Fuck the Star!
Fuck the Star! Fuck the Star! Fuck the Star! Fuck the Star-r-r-r!"
my grandmother looking embarrassed
as Janice dances past
snapping her fingers high in the air and singing loud
so nobody could miss the words
my grandmother
stiffening like cukes in alum
her deer face a disapproving wince
as if the words were hitting her
each like a twinge in the spine
but Allen Ginsberg
he was a willow by a river
who couldn't help
but feel the wind
while his roots ran under the water
and he reached for the painted sun
in a painted sky like an hypnotic peach
he believed he could pick
and if he swallowed it
with his belly full of light
and his head as warm
as a stone in bed
he'd solve the world and give us all
the name of the dance
he danced.

I Want to Swim in your Liverpool

Oh, I want to swim in your Liverpool
dive into
the water of dream
sleep, wake, remember,
return from drowning—
down
where the walls sweat in the Cavern Club
in the harbour clank
of a city
where the Canard Yank
smoked
in the heat and noise
with drainies and winkle pickers
and cheap guitars
(on this difficult planet
there are wonderful things
we cannot share
speaking, listening...
the heart of a body in dance
races to the edge of a cliff—
looks)
            and
            outside the closed parenthetic of beating ribs

j

u

m

p

s

.

.

.

My Mother Brought Home a Record

Ours was a home of country tunes
my grandfather
clutching the wafer thin disk
from the latest Geographic
and cranking the box
like a weird monkeyless hurdy gurdy
the needle's long inoculation
dropping into the oily pool of grooves
that spun the voice alive and played
in some tropic zone
and it played my father's honky tonk
and my mother's hooki lau
and my father's Lumbardo phase
and it played the drunken tones of cowboy angst
and it played the sweet laments of dead Jim Reeves
who died before I heard him sing,
"Put your sweet lips
 a little closer to the phone"
and it played the exiled Nova Scotian twang of Hank Snow
sounding to me then
like a cat being killed
in the kitchen,
but my mother must have seen
how I came in close
to the cheap cream-coloured radio
that sat staticy on top of the fridge
how I turned the volume up
to catch the Beatles
on CFCO out of Chatham
as important to me as the war broadcasts had been to her

for my mother's hair
was strangely sprinkled with stars
where she mined in the kitchen
with fruit pies and peaches cut in half
on the table like a gold-panner's moons.

This is the Phone

This is the phone that rings
like a two-tag dog scratching a flea.
This is the phone
that falls like a stiff crow
from the shoulder it can't quite grip.
This is the phone
that heard my father's words,
"Dad's gone," then the quiet weeping
like rain blown off the glass.
And this is the phone
that heard my pocms first—
my sister reading them like shared recipes
for making jam,
those precious bad Beatle verses of mine
Ringo-pingo-ing
like rotten roulette
with me breathless outside the door:
a spy in the house.
And this is the phone I "Britished"
when it was cool
to impress my cousins
because the sixties belonged to England
and I
belonged to the sixties.
This is the phone
that told how Tom had died
peacefully in the night
his life, like colour leaving apples
alone too long in the dark.
And this is the phone
that brings my sister home
three thousand miles away
and me, living in Bell city,
I hear my mother's voice
like sea breeze in a conch,
my father's voice

21

slow as the drain of water
from laundry on a line
slow as the change that sunlight brings
to photosynthetic spring
telling me there are funerals to attend
and I cannot look at this phone
without hearing voices shrink.

The Obsession

When I was a boy
I learned to eat with my left hand
bought a tin silver
identification bracelet
inscribed Paul by a gypsy with a jittery drill
and I practised the flowing signature

Paul McCartney

until I could duplicate it
like a bank forgery
in my cheap green Dent School Dictionary
haunted by ink and
as if I were a frail
boy copyist trapped by poverty
into toiling over figures
Ms. Fordbed cracked my fingers like kindling
to change the script
because I scrawled and blotted
fainting into bloody accusation
as she bent breathing and yeasty
over my desk
her huge arms heaving my hand
into an uneven cursive
so each word changed
like some committee of liars composing notes
through the crucible
of my feckless arms
pushed by the will of ghosts
though I found my way

and threw my dreams
beyond the farm
beyond the fleshy obstacle or her patterning two loaf arms
beyond the simple minded lines
of early work
refusing to counterfeit the wild boy
in britches
clapped in a wooden desk.

When People Believed Beatle Music Grew Better Radishes

Before history had spoiled the future.
Before it lay metamorphosed with murder
and an ugly incomprehensible
jungle war
when people believed
that Beatle music grew
better radishes
or so Lynn Bashkov proved
to her father in New York
where their tumescent tip roots
throbbed "She Loves You" deep into shallow living-room soil
like lonely husbands in hotels.
With their measure and remeasure
of sunlight dripping
old paint thick on their rose walls
while the aphid
looked at its hands
and considered the absence of ants
a tiny farmer in an empty barn
built from silk scraps
green and red
still
she watched while her own breasts swelled
like breathing birds
and boys hatched hair
the gathering of dry grass
that goes gray
as singe then white
as the first October frost
when we begin to lose
our fathers, hold our mothers
dear and doddering
old dogs staggered by sharp noises.

And I remember
when it hadn't happened yet
before each mothy moon
was cut from attic lace in a circle
then snipped away by madness
and the need to work
when gulls settled and resettled
in familiar fields
with a hundred broken seasons
that invented themselves took inventory
and weeds declined into snow then collapsed
like white worn-out wicker snapped by weight.

And where is she now
this griefless girl
who mothered her crop
married science to music
till the juke box noise
exhausted its groove
and wore away her youth
in revolutions
that never failed by staying the same.

Tom Malott and Bob Dylan

The hired man
Tom didn't like the Beatles much
but when I played Dylan
he came from his room
leaving behind the clock-oil smells
the cigar smoke
hanging like tea steam above his bed
and crept into the music
(a cat coming out for milk)
the tentative wool-sock shuffle
the shifting of his new bib overalls
the material like light-gage tin stiffened at the cuffs
hands in his pockets
as if he meant to turn them out for straw
his small smile
pink-gummed and toothless
the watery tobacco-coloured eyes
one rogue
tilting at the ceiling a little
he asked, "who's that?" of
Dylan's smoker's voiced
"she makes love just like a woman,
but she breaks
just like a little girl"
with the breathy harmonica
wheezing above the acoustic guitar in another song.
"I like him," he says. "He's good."
And I almost see Tom
sitting in sessions, in his room,
taking his mouth organ,
tapping the keys for spit
and playing this whole damn poem
into silence.

A Stippled Ceiling Was the Heaven of My Youth

Linoleum chrysanthemums my earth.
The window of my little world
opened to a garden
and beyond that to cow pasture
and beyond that the train
that shook the fence rows
like a lousy bull rubbing his hip.

From my four walls
the fanzine Beatles
were guardian angels
who fluttered when you walked
and pulled against their tacks
like the tug of buttons when you tuck in a shirt.
And there was Quiet George
with his sunburst Gretch guitar
and sad-eyed Richard
his hands jewelled and gaudy
like eight melted crayons
and rye, hawk-nosed John, his half grin
sarcastic even in silence
and posing Paul, using the camera
stepping into and through the lens
bending light, sustaining the shape of the note
in two dimensions.
These four paper men
who peopled my youth
trembling like polite applause
or the ripple of opening sails
in still waters
whenever you touched the door.
These secular saints
I worshiped, my father wincing
like a mouth full of hot unsweetened lemon,
my mother organizing her response
like tea service

outside my room
tinkled in with laundry smells
but I was the only dog
who saw the ghost.
They were dumb and deaf
I dropped the needle in the groove
and God pressed his ear to the house
like a person
with a music box that won't open
though it plays
a lovely tune.

Twist and Shout at the 4H Club

All of us were there at the year-end rally:
boys with lambs, wethers and ewes,
girls with calves, heifers and steers,
guys with pigs, barrows and sows,
chicks with chickens, capons and hens,
dolls with horses, fillies and gelds,
and even the cakey Kates
and bread-breasted Brendas
weaving and sewing and baking
sweet smelling with dough-white hands
and seams in cloth travelling the Singer stitch
in a gingham stream
our fathers with twine burns on their palms
where they'd twanged the bales
like bass guitars lifted by their strings
their jackknives shut in their pockets
their wooden matches ear-waxed on the tip
shining in their shirt breasts
with the fire folded in
our mothers smelling of purse perfume
and mothy wool
shifting in their girdles
with the hysterical silence of repressed humanity
so that when our leaders
came to the stage in Beatle wigs
dropped the needle into Twist and Shout
and mocked the music with their kitchen brooms
I looked around the room
and saw the energy draining like a plug-pulled sink
into this crowd
and thought of how the cows will leave the field
and plod for barns when they are full of milk.

The Summer I Bought Beatle Boots in Detroit

No more rushing the rivers of otherwise empty roads
we crossed the border
humming into the viaducts of the city
emerging slow, as if we were knitting our way
through woolly air
rumpled above the buildings.
We walked from the parking lot into the cattle-drive crowds
thick in the street beside Hudsons
where I bought a copy of Revolver
Voorman's fish-eye lens rendering
in black and white lines and weird
druggy featured narrow faces
book of the dead and Hollywood acid lyrics
sunshine sitar and cello lonely women
transition I only notice now.
And I bought a pair of Wellingtons,
winkle pickers like the Beatles wore
to be photographed in baby carriages
beside phone booths
in Liddypool in 64.
What a crazy quilt this life.
I remember invisible things
and sew them
with threads of sound
into a great design
like the day I tripped through Ridgetown High
in the glossy brick floor halls of that old school
or the day I tossed them
in the trash
because their cuban heels
were crooked with so much walking
that I would have seemed drunk
a very stagger of goats
driven mad by the dogs of the mind.

The Summer of Love

I was listening to the drift of Pepper
and looking at legs
when most of the girls I knew
weren't used to their new breasts yet
glancing down
at their bodies softening
and the gentle swell of their hips
when they walked
seemed with the sway
to flow inside their skirts
the light and colour changing as they moved
the way a footprint stains the strand
and seeps away.
And I could drink the memory of their going then
as canvas takes and keeps its paint
even in darkening rooms.
But now I and my lifelong love
spend our summers by the lake
with our two boys breathing larger
every year
I feel strangely sad
where once within the vigour of my youth I would have
spun the hands of clocks like bingo dials
and pushed the sun ahead to see horizons change
I long to catch each moment
as a leaf will catch the wind
and move with it awhile before it lets it loose
for there is a season coming
when my innocent boys will begin
to notice girls.

When I Was in Love with D....

the paint was still wet on the world
and the sky liquid blue
yet I would have thrown all moral rules
into chaos
to have dreamed her womb
like David.
I would have betrayed my inheritance
bad father, evil brother, corrupted king,
I would have beggared the haberdasher
of all his blackest hats
I would have kissed my master for a dime
and hung around
like a wedding guest
with my own woebegone story to tell.
I would have defigged and fallen from grace..
disappled like Sir Isaac Newton's epiphany
coming rotten from the bough
my vinegary funk
spreading the stain of contagion on the barrel rounding
of his forehead.

But I was still a boy
and in a week it seems
as with the transient desire of Romeo for his Rosaline
I lost the need to counterfeit my heart
and surrendered one sweet madness
for another,
but in all those years
I took no poisons, gave no neighbours grief.
Now, like a lucky priest,
I look to give advice.

The Sergeant Pepper Sonnets

i

Remember how you wanted her
falling/backwards into your bed
her skirt flowing/into her body shapes
like warm butter/
while you listened to Sergeant Pepper
the/summer you were sixteen
and the music/moved in your skull
like the moods of smoke
when/twenty years seemed
such a long time and
John/Lennon's first son was a school boy
dreaming/diamonds.
Or the gravel road dust fuming/up
behind your uncle's truck
and you heard/"A Day in the Life"
in the blue cab
and/if anyone had changed the station
then/you'd have killed them
and struck out all
alone/because you believed in love
and music.

ii

When Sixteen magazine ran the last fan/zene photographs
of the fab four in six/tyseven
mustachioed and gone to/grass
with the piccolo trumpet on Pen/ny Lane
and the swoozing organ rhythms/
of Strawberry Fields
two cool tree leaps a/way
from the bubble gum and braces set/
they left behind
the pre-pubescent or/ganisms
called "screaming girls" and took up/
the red roach and hookah water
bubbling/hot like dangerous chemistry
and/ the Technicolour wash of a
psylocy/bin sunset the way the sea shares itself
/with the sky becoming cobalt blue:

you either drown or learn to swim;
you either fall or learn to fly.

iii

I was just getting over my sister/ singing
in the house like a shower
full/ of girl scouts when the radio
matured/ and the lamp cooled
like a child's forehead com/ing out of fever
and the rooms went gloom/y
with artificial shade
and the meat/smells of a shared harvest
long after we'd/lost
the wheat-gold hair of childhood
and gone/ to work in sweat-shops,
fast-food chicken joints/and the hot
fields of my father's bean rows/
where we followed the planter's graph like tough/
philosophical arguments easy/
to lose involving why those pulled weeds
sagged/ in our hands
like the failure of desire.

iv

my own Sergeant Pepper salad of snap/shots
would include Hitler and Curly How/ard
grandfather Lee and Tom the hired/ man
stuck there like two straw-infected dolls/
their pant cuffs leaking
the viscera of/ harvest barns,
the many masked Beatle boys,/ Dylan
Thomas and so many poets/
they would seem a heavy crop
of faces/ on a halloween shop wall
we'd never/ wear them out wearing
them out
and of course,/ Holden, the hopeless
catcher whom I read/
trapping the light in my own upstairs
hall/ coming in at the window like a
thief/ of words—the winter afternoon
the all-American assassin.

I Was Spreading Manure in the Summer of Love

I was spreading manure
in the summer of love
and it fell on my cap
like a movie-set rain
and I smelled of the world
and I smelled of a green-thumb garden
of the black earth
beneath the rose
and I was in tune with the field
like a dog near a hole he can't find
where mice live
and I roamed like the wind in the wheat
and leaving a swath
like a boat in the sea
where the grass crushed brown
in my wake
while the tug went light on the tongue
and the wheels rode the ruts
where ground hogs lived
and the cattle tree
wove its leaves for the breeze
like a woman with sheets from the wash she can't hold
and I was in love
with the beauty of girls
I saw even in the whisper of clouds
as they came down to sleep in the blue
trailing gowns of vapour vacant white
and sometimes then
if I held the sun in my mind
behind closed eyes
all thinking went warm and full of thin yellow light
and life was so good I could dream
it was real.

Fight with Uncle J.

The night just before he invaded my room
I'd slipped the record on
and jacked the volume
"Hey Jude" and flip-side "Revolution"
the guitar fuzz
stirring the dust beneath the bed
like the breath of a ram breathing
into his own wool.
At first he rapped on the door
as if I were some
domestic dispute he'd come to quiet
and I
did not let him in.
The second time he knocked
so the spike heads in the wall studs jumped
and I
did not let him in.
The third time
he came bursting through the door
like a bull
the larger geometries of his manhood
held in check
I stood my ground
my own little adolescent fulcrums full of jittery angles
we squared ourselves up
like a shelf of leaning books
and the fight was on.

There was no roughing.
No blows were struck,
though the window shook its glass a little
with the bass notes
we turned around the moment
like a pair of tethered-together dogs
and he released me
from the wolf-grip of his eyes

backed away and cooled the air
with an autumn draft
a brief scuffle of leaves kicked up
and the music drained away
between us
for seven years.

Walter Cronkite's Deep Voice

tells me the moon
belongs to America
and I believe
they own some fifty stars
mapped on the clothy horoscope
of an inky blue night
too, and what the oil kings
have moiled from the desert world
from the squeezed down
distilled and slippery troglodites
that drive the engines of the realm
they own these and
the huge creaking forests crackling
full of paper
and the foamy chemical sludge
of inter city rivers
and the oceans
boiling against the lunar pull
leaving their scraps on the shore
like a picnic
driven indoors by rain
but back to the moon
that big cheese fermenting in the heavens
full of holes
inoculated by rockets
and claimed like a lyon's club door prize.
Let's drag it home
and eat it all
while we watch a movie.

Deep Readers

For all the deep readers
who find Christ
millipeding under every 20th
character of the alphabetagameron
the air thick with magnificats
crawling up Calvary
like the wet underside
of a potato board...
read this poem backwards
and you will find
"I buried Paul, if 28
 I am the Walrus-impostor
 fool on the hill
 who blew his mind out in a car
 crossing Abby Road
 sans zapatos!" Like slugs in soil
I'm lost
in the deepening exegesis of handsome grass.

Riding to Orangeville with John Lennon in my Head

Struck
by how young I was
and given to unprovoked levitation
floating
above the landscape
like the seed-blown angels
of a dandelion crop
I guess I must have been
riding to Orangeville
with John Lennon in my head
tasting the wind
the way dogs do
with their faces stuck out of pick-up truck windows
the sun on the horizon
like the best Florida orange
I ever saw
with the whole day rolling out
blue cloth
just for me
and some fields breathed fresh-cut hay
and June
was happening every moment
for the rest of the month
while the voice of the song "Imagine"
the deep, resonant piano chords
and all that refused reality
were mine alone
until I came upon the borders
of the town—
the pretty little fences
the thorny guard of roses, the gravity of blossoms
improving week by week.

I Was a Green Boy with Those
White Room Blackbird Red Neck Purple Haze Blues

And I had an Afro
that would fill a door
and I wore
always open and floating because the buttons wouldn't hold
an indigo blue Canadian air force great-coat
with huge mother-knitted mittens
the colour of thistles
at the height of summer
and I wore a long purple scarf
trailing at the throat
like Goethe skating in Germany
and I wore
pink bell-bottom trousers
and flowered shirts
and I was the Brummel of weird
I was the tangled garden of winter
I was the quintessential manifestation of music
I was the Sturm und Drang
of an orchard in storm
enough to rattle the ladders
and dump the pails
and I was as full of poems
as Dylan Thomas's grave
and we sat in the cafeterias of the seventies
and spoke like muses
over coffee and beer
and we were all promise and wish
with flesh like silk
and wild minds that took to the wind
like the white whip of snow
and John Kennedy died and Malcolm X died
and Martin Luther King died
and Bobby Kennedy died
and Al Wilson died

and Jimi Hendrix died
and Jim Morrison died
and John Lennon died
and Ronald Reagan didn't
but we never gave in to grief
with nothing to regret
when poets had voices
and people had ears.

Jimi Hendrix in the Company of Cows

i

Mooooooo
          oooOOoooOoo

    oOoOo
         o

      o
    OOOOOOOOOOOOOO
                  o
                    oOo

OoOoOoOo

mmmmmmmmmmmmmmmMMMMMMMMMMMMMMMo
oooooooo

oooooooooooooooooooooooOOOOOOO

OOOOOOOOOOOOOOO

mm ooo   mm ooo mm oo

                mmmmmmmmmmmmmmmmmmoooooooooo

                                    n

ii

Listening to the Band of Gypsies
in my bedroom
while the cows maul their calves
like all day suckers
sticky bulls-eyed clockwork springs of red roan hair
that swirl like soft ice cream
Machine gun chords
strafing the fence line, music drifting
out the window, out over the cattle
maple tree shakes
and fastens the
sky
to the edge of the barn, heifer works an itch, stamps
off   flies, Jimi ride his red guitar
over all sniping pebbles into whirls of air
New Year's Eve, 1969, photographs on fire
the same summer I sit on the edge of my bed
with flames in my hair
cows outside—lifting their jaws from the grass
pause to consider
as if they smelled smoke.

iii

First year University
I Electric Lady-Landed my roommate too much
so one day he came in
like an operant-conditioning chicken
playing a wall of lights
bantam rooster strutting
lifting the needle from the groove
so it made that telltale
"zzzzreeeeeekkkk!" I cannot spell
and 1983 a Merman I Should Turn to Be was never the same
after that, skipping in the drum beat
an erratic cardiogram, Mitch Mitchell losing sight of his
hands, stumbling into his drum kit
like a strip joint punch line...
some would say it was the stale-sweet marijuana smell
in my jacket
and some would blame the recreational alphabet
I consumed like language in the dreamscapes of Chagall
but for one year I dove into the music
into the black concentric pools of vinyl
into the stereophonic roulette
the sound swirling in the headphones
like a marble in a milk pail
from the September he died
til the terrible ice-cube bath hot June in Paris
til my father came to me
telling me I was no good, in the bull yard summer
the smell of manure high in the air
miles from the edge of the world.

Bad Reception

I remember watching
television when
its unfixed picture
sent striped faces shooting
above the set
the forehead rolling under the chin
implicating a stack of tumbled heads
in a liberated village
too far from the centre of civilization
for anyone to care
about the loss of intelligence
or the death of good hands.
Any night
in the middle of a movie
in the middle of the best
breathless moment
when Marilyn rolled her hips in a chair
and crossed her legs
like the flowing together of cream and milk
if the weather changed
swirling the static heavens
so the clouds crowded and tore
and moonlight's moods grayed
and the cathode snows
subsumed all shapes and forms
and the screen went hoar
with an electric shroud
so you spilled your chips
scrambling up to adjust the sky
shaking the flurries in a bauble
and blinking off the blur
of a sleepy swoon.
And then you whacked the wood
to jar the tubes
as they shimmered and fuzzed
like shook green flies

that carried New York on their wings
bringing Miss America dancing in
disguised as some amateur hour majorette
who knocks her baton button on the floor
like the graceless genuflection of a knob-kneed girl
in silver tights
not like now
as we satellite irrelevance, distraction,
deception, and the generalized
obfuscation of the real
so clear
it shines all night from black to black
in certain houses
aspontaneousfire
intheheartofheapsofcoal
thetrueeventburiedsofarbeneaththesurface
theinfernalintoxicationseemsdistant
coolandinsouciantaswouldthebirthofanyotherall-consuming

star.

Finding the source of silence

The first time ever
the room went strange
we fled
bumping together like birthdays
all the way down the stairs
from floor six upper
chasing noise
and full of bells my limbs
swam air
as a dog's will held fast six inches above the water line
the stairs went
Eschering on in dreamy forevers
convinced
by never arriving at doors
that some mad artist
had touched his pencil
to the building
then   we rushed outside
into the dead-cool touch of a November night
looking at the moon
like the light still wet in a pale yellow jar
we followed the road
till we found the source of silence
and dressed in our sweet-smelling coats
we called to our mothers...a hundred miles away...
we are lost, we are lost, we are lost...

A Writer's Warning

I warn you now
that after you die
I will tell all your
dark secrets
and
people will say
this was his life
and I will invent lies
to replace you
and people will wonder
was he really so bad
and friends will say
is it possible
that we knew him so little
that his true heart
was so sick?
And I will show them
the iodine stain of the scars you left
on your children
and they will weep
and remember nothing
and their tears
will shame your grave
like salt rain.

And I will broadcast
your worst moments
your greatest failures
your most cruel indulgences
your least admired accomplishments.
I will confirm sordid suspicions
concerning drugs, alcohol, and naked little girls
in late night hotel-room shadows.
I will remain silent
in the face of ill-conceived accusations
too horrible to contemplate.

I will celebrate innuendo
and exaggerate
your faults
so that excited fools become expert biographers
and make a parlour game
of false memory.
And your most decorous enemies will curse you lightly
in polite conversations
with whispered invective
and your photograph
will be a bull's eye in bars
and people will wear
unforgiving silk-screens
of your sleazy image
and everyone will acknowledge
that your time on the earth
was one long lost weekend
under a streetlamp
where it always drizzles
and even good matches are hard to light.

A Hanky, a Piece of Fruit, and a Word

Peter came home
calmly gripping his fruit
and reciting his mantra
he sat catatonic in his chair
like remembered sleep
never mind the pass Nigel
had made in the tent in New Orleans
sending him scrambling north
disturbed to report how he'd been startled awake
by Nigel's hand sliding like a snake in shifting silver
never mind the day
he'd been caught grifting drugs
and been beaten by thugs
with knuckles like lug nuts
and faces whittled from logs
never mind how they'd taken him
cruising in black
while their low-down voices oozed out thick with threat
like an oil change full of grit
how he'd winced for an hour after
setting his bruised chin
on his palm
like a peach too soft to eat
twisting his wounded arm in its sleeve
like a crooked curtain rod
now he had
reason enough to anaesthetize memory
and move
into the zen
that flowed through his mind
like an autumn river
silting wide and shallow over sand.

When Gerry Mathers Died in Vietnam

When the Beaver died in Vietnam
we imagined his chopper going down fluttering and wild-winged
like a blackbird shot in a swamp
while Ward Cleaver was wise for days in our dreams
quietly pacing the cloudy rugs
outside an empty ethereal room
addressing the knob of the door
with his hand almost landing
like a gull in a draft
his slack trousers
billowing their cuffs to tickle his dacks
because he wants to give advice
to the ghost of a glove
and the angel of a vacant cap
tossed swivelling on the stile of a chair like the brainy quoits
of a bored boy, but he can't
remember his lines written to deal with the pointless harmony
of people lost in war
gone missing from lives so long you forget their faces.
And then, there's Wally, grooming for grief
weeping like an onion cutter
cutting onions slow and close to the eyes
while June cooks in the kitchen
feeling how warm the cold lemons come
from the false frigedare
how the wrap stays shut on the lunch bags so long
the muffins mould and go the beautiful blue of a woman's bruise
how the roast smells
like paper
how the cake falls in the pan
and the coffee cups drop
wormy from their hooks.
Oh, then, then there is the awful
lonely look of the street
saying, "why is the grass still so green
and why is the boulevard hushed

with huge and dreamy trees
full of quiet birds?——-
never mind the myth of facts—
that we were wrong enough
to live to see
Gerry Mathers short and stout
a mere man again.

Cartesian TV? or What the Camera Confirms

They see themselves
sitting on stage
craning their necks to see
an image
of themselves
craning their necks to see
themselves
sitting on stage
craning their necks to see
an image of themselves.

Let Me Share this Tale

Let me share this tale
of shamed blue faces
lost in blue light
the blue-white of the blue-white milk of blue Dutch cows
while we fall from grace
with oil-slick angels
plunging through pools of night
where we tumble
like wedding-cake grooms
and give our wasted bodies to the wind
moving through clouds
faces taking the shape of shrouds

Let me share this tale
of the suicide of sisters...
Let me kiss those toad cold lips
I haul with slimy buckets
clapping up the sides
of wishing wells.

A Poem Concerning the Attempted Assassination of Ronald Reagan

It wasn't exactly Squeaky From
with her little gun
in the tight crowd around Gerald Ford
and it certainly wasn't a conspiracy of agents
configured on a grassy knoll
in Dallas
and it certainly wasn't the tragic death
of greatness
I witnessed the afternoon I was driving to hockey
shamed by a moment of hope
when I heard the news on the radio
and that night I saw
the body guards draping the chief
within their angel wing trench coat shoulders
like hawks eating yellow chickens on the nightly news
while Jim Brady
fell with a tiny hole in his brain
and all the excited gun shots were popping off
like fire crackers
tied to the tail of a crippled dog.

Then we saw the would-be assassin, over and over again
proclaiming his private desire
to impress movie star Jodi Foster.
And this is what we'd come to in the trickle down years:
(The pimple faced science major
dreaming of a date with a beauty queen
kills his mother while she sleeps.
Ridiculous lonely losers
leaf through gun catalogues
their heartbeats going quick as scissors
in lingerie.
Loveless silver screen tough guys
leaping from great heights
with sweet delights
melting in their arms
like corn butter gone soft in the sun
these fainting pools of blonde women
dumbly lifted into beds
while weirdos play dead circles
in empty rooms
that smell of navy beans
and wet weather.)

"Too bad John Hinkley wasn't a better shot!"
a friend of mine says to me
tired of the government of money
tired of the false and chimerical third-world wars
while a mad little nerd
his heavy black spectacles sliding down his nose
fingers the trigger of his cheap revolver
walks into our kitchen
and blows us both away
like dust from old books.

The Nihilistic Beatle

She doesn't love you.
Na! Na! Na!
She doesn't love you.
Na! Na! Na!
She doesn't love you.
Na! Na! Na! Naaaa!

Well, I saw her yesterday
and
she didn't tell me
any thi-a-ing...
                          except
she doesn't love you
so....
Fuck off
and shut up!

Weeping for Henry

I never wept for Thomas.
I never wept for Richard.
I never wept for Henry.
I never wept for all those lost relations
who faded from photographs
like the slow dimming of faces
in movie houses
though I sensed their going
as in the excited stillness of children
hiding into dark.
And when the doctor followed a heartbeat
to some grim conclusion
in the human silence so huge
it filled a little body space
that once held the universe
he seemed at first like someone straining to hear
the weather on a cheap radio
and if you felt nothing in the mortality of others
who could blame you
for not grieving at the strangeness
and who can blame for your weeping now
with death becoming so familiar.

Correcting Reality

Consider if you will
a post-modernist face.

The aquiline queerness of its nose.
The angular line
of the cheeks.
Flesh, the weird colour
of my grandfather's separated cream
suffering
 technique
  perspective
   angst in art.

Narcissus is
drowning
in glass
(the hundred thousand
tricks of light)
see   how coming close
life almost always declar/ifies
the living, other.

Catullus' Madonna

image
       milkweed, peach, gourd
peeled pear, sour cherry
lady slipper, pink rose
bruised apple
crushed fern, wet web

image
       mushroom, asparagus,
nettle stalk, young
plums, walnuts
worm flux in wet soil

image
the snail has slimed the silk.

image
the silk receives the snail.

Funny Violence and Cartoon Dreams

I want to say to my sons:
"...if you promise to imagine,
    I'll promise to remember..."

But false memory
and desultory dreams
intervene

and I become
the raging curmudgeon
mistaking fashion for disrespect
and you become
the slouches I fear
loose with language
acting at life
as if every sidewalk were a stage
and all the sideshow video clowns
were paradigms to print your coins
and palm your faces.

And it gets to be about
haircuts, somehow.
And it gets to be about
trousers and hats
and the sartorial wars
that divide father from child
and the two-legged tipping of dining room chairs
seems important.
And because I long to save you
from the funny violence
and cartoon dreams
of a culture gone mad
never mind
my fuzzy afro that used to fill a door
never mind
the danger in the wilds of being young

I've learned something
and I want you to ignore
the way I learned it.
I've salvaged some truths
from the rubble of experience.
No need to repeat my mistakes my sons.
Believe me
even as you
move into the world
like two small fragile boats
leaving the still stream
casting your paddles
into the open waters of this shared sun-bright lake.

Please Finish Reading this Poem

She is twelve
and overwhelmed by hormones
her body
metamorphosing before your eyes
as if it were slowly filling with air
(I struggle here
against the erotic, but
I swear)
she flirts her small breasts
spreading her arms back and open
like a seagull landing on a post
and with the vague insinuations
of a sleepy cat
she stretches and arches
teasing as if she meant to dance at any moment
a dance of veils
whisping in doorways like candle smoke
from candles snuffed in church.
And she moves weaving vapours
like the last few seconds of something
being suffocated by ether.

Yesterday she was a child.
Her father drank too much.
Her mother swore
and threw the sugar bowl
across the room
so it cracked against the wall
and went "clup" as hollow empty bowls always will
the sugar leaving a shiny trail
of pyxie dust
as if Tinker Bell had taught blind crockery to fly.
And so in violence and rage they gave her up
to strangers and she
went from house to house
like the Avon Lady's wild and lonely daughter.

Hear how in every neighbourhood she crosses
the cold water taps are running
to cool the fever in fathers and sons
who are crowding into shower stalls
their manhood drooping
like marigolds in a heavy rain.
See how her teacher
smooths his brow with ice
as if she were mercury running the glass too fast.

But she is helpless as a cut rose
blooming too early in aspirin and stale water.
She gives away her colour
her deep red velvet petals
dying in the artificial light.

How to Flatter the Dead: An Instruction on Popular Art in the Second Half of the Twentieth Century

There is Elvis' only surviving
illegitimate son's idea...
his hair boufed like foaming black meringue
his silver lamé shirt shaking with his ample belly
like a shook sheet
of aluminium oven foil shaped around a twenty dollar picnic ham
while his belt buckle beggars
all the best bronco riders and
wrestle-maniacs ever cinched their trousers
with a prize
and as he croons his larynx is
rising and falling
to the slither of silk scarves
and he does the kind of bump and grind
to make Ed Sullivan
disinter his coffin
the rotten boards bursting through the soil
his bones levitating like someone fixing the horizontal hold
on paradise.

And there is Jim Morrison
growing lordly, fat, and icy in Paris
like a polar Narcissus lowering his body into water
more beer cooler for hockey players than bath
so his heart stops beating
like a squeezed bird
and he becomes legend
leonine, half-naked, drunk, drugged poet.
And masters of cartoon literature
begin scribbling on the lavatory walls
of America.
And incompetent Michelangelos
begin chipping away at his tombstone
dreaming his corrupted face from the rock.

And there is John Lennon
canonized: Saint Winston O. Boogie
his humanity crucified
on a cross-hatch 22
ergo: the hagiography of music.
ergo: the hagiography of money.
there goes the humanity of men.

And Jimi...he's alive
whippet thin and bald
as any closet corpse
singing Viva Las Vegas
in the Nevada Nirvana
burning his axe
for slot-machine grannies
humping his speakers
for farmers on furlow
while the queens of blue rinse
faint like swamp vapours into pools of their own costume pearls
while Janis warbles in the wings
singing, "Feelings" with curly poodles swaddled in her arms
like her favourite fox fur stole.

To Ferne Halwes Kowthe in Sondry Londes*

"Tobias has been rather amusing, telling tales of his recent trip to Europe—
..."the pilgrimage"—visiting the grave of Jim Morrison at the Pere Lachaise*
cemetery in Paris: 'it was super easy to find. People had spray painted
This way to Jimmy's all over the tombstones of all these dead French poets.
It was great."

from Generation X

Within the lyghted towne without a care
Laye the helpless bones of poet Baudelaire
Where lyke a signe upon a milestone writ
It is to showe the palmer where the martyr sits.
And there the ghost of each poem gone
Is beacon-blacke as Rimbaud's opium.
And in the time of Aprille blossom springe
When book and brook and bird and lovers singe
Then come the tourist and the wild pilgrim
To visit at the tombe of hero Jim
Leaving everywhere their marks and evidence
Upon the walk of stones; upon the graveyard fence
With broken dreams that smell of whiskey drinkers
And sacramental malt that stains where urine tinkers
While smoke that ryses from the sullen saintly faces
Changes everything as fog will foggy places
And to the shrine they come as to a Door
Open in the skye through which they pour
Like angels with soote smelling clothes
Their fingers soiled with soil they wipe their nose
As bending down like flowers in the wind
They pay their homage to the fallen mind
While each sad poet suffers such neglect
His words forgotten though they were perfect
Laforge, Nerval, Verlaine, do not compare
For them the only lizard king is buried there.

*To distant shrines known in sundry lands
  from Chaucer's "General Prologue" to Canterbury Tales

The Old Man at the Jimi Hendrix Movie

The old man
at the Jimi Hendrix Movie
dodders away from the screen
as is he were
cut from drab cloth
fashioned from shadowy
and inarticulate spider spun
gummy gray webs.
He canes his way slow
up the slope of the aisle
about ninety
and lost, he seemed lost
with twelve foot Jimi
in his fire-red silks
stretching the strings so the amps wailed
and his beautiful black face
suffered the blues
and spoke the kind of lovely fluid hurt
the voice in his fingers was meant to speak
but the old man walks away
cranking his knees
for slow purchase
as if his pockets were full of worthless pebbles
and he wanted to steal them
while he was still alive.

I'm Sick of These Times

I'm sick of the sleazy
empathy of talk shows.
I'm sick of seeing
Phil Donohue in a dress.
I'm sick of seeing
Opera Winfree crying.
I'm sick of my own generation
addicted to recovery
and blaming their parents
for the angst they feel
at middle age
disappointed with their toys and gadgets
suffering the spiritual hunger
of empty lives.
I'm sick of Geraldo's
amazing cross-dress nazi punks
and I'm sick of Charlie Manson's madness.
I'm sick of simulated reality.
I'm sick of the gutter press.
I'm sick of the movie of the week.
I'm sick of books written by criminals.
I'm sick of the tawdry lives of the rich and famous.
I'm sick of the Prime Minister.
I'm sick of the Prince of Whales.
I'm sick of stories concerning strumpets.
I'm sick of bare breasted women
marching on Guelph.
I'm sick of the abortion wars.
I'm sick of learning secrets.
I'm sick of the word "fuck".
I'm sick of angry inner city poor
posing in the midst of gold and muscle.
I'm sick of the distractions.
I long to put my hand to the breast of the earth
but like some sad shadow
I withdraw touching nothing.

Wonderbread Wrapper

easy rhymes and facile rhythms
full of anger, angst and gism
suburban rot and urban schism
inner city dithyrambs
writ on golden pentagrams
pent up sling@slang poems
of righteous power, violence
poverty and decadence
vulgar language and offense
say yes to drugs cause school's a drag
say yes to booze and dope and brag
to cocaine, crack, and horse and skag
say yes to guns and early chill
say yes to gangs who drive by kill
through force of habit, force of will
for dukes and dudes and studs are cool
while losers lose and colours rule
but white boy is a white boy, fool
his poems stutter stammer mute
to ballyrags who swagger boot
from papal bull to cartoon cute
with sample tunes and drum machines
backward hats and stone-washed jeans
and running shoes for TV screens
he'd rather die in death with pogue
than live to wear a banker's brogue
cause strut is strut, and rogue's in vogue.

The John Lennon Angel

The John Lennon Angel
came fluttering down spastic
into a dream of night
like a sparrow
stunned by a stone.
Made weird pained faces as he landed hard on the yard
and swearing like a priest who breaks his ankles
in the funny papers.

"It's a goddamn long way from heaven!"
he said
squeezing his guitar
in through the open window going, "bump, bump, twang!"
as he thumped the ledge
broke the glass
like a thief going backwards.

Then he sang, standing, bouncing a little
his legs akimbo on the bed
and while he sang
a half-distracted tune
the happy dog of the house licked his knee caps
like broken eggs
and the cat, purring
swatted at his heart place
sniffing his feathers
dreaming with a big appetite
because wet with fog
and cloud dew he resembled a huge human dove
dipped in milk.

"I've had enough of paradise," he sang
the bullets dropping from his ribs
like heavy tears.
"I've hade enough of that dying fame."
And his wings spread open ragged
as pillows ripped with knives
and he flew beyond the window
like a gull with a guitar.

The Substitution

I could stand all day
on this wave-wounded shore
watch the sun rise and arc
in a slow serve
hear the pebbles mumble and move
mumble and move
the lake like a bored gold panner
looking for only the best blue glass
while the water line rubs the rusty dock dark
and the large stones
set themselves against their green beards
and jaw like the half-talk of thinkers' chins
and one canoe makes a lazy copulation
with its anchor in the sand.
Later a bronzed and boozy moon
will seep through the heavens
like a wet lemon in a paper towel
and every star
will glow with inhaled fire
but no one will make a movie
to prove it happened
as American President Kennedy's skull
blew apart in Zapruterized reality
like a nut struck by a bat
and we all said,
"yes, there it is, see,
I can see the blood on Jackie's dress!"
as she crawls
across the trunk of the car
scrambling to avoid the sudden grave
mocked by panic
and the ineluctable lens
and we have the grassy knoll
burned in our shaky frames
we can freeze the moment better than memory
replace the heart of the story
so it makes better lawyers of us all
giving cold consideration
to the facts that make up our lives.

The Day I wrote My First Poem

I tasted the rain, it tasted of dust, wet dust.
I felt the snow freeze hot
on my face.
I smelled the rich smell of manure
on the wind of my father's fall farm
and the summer smell of wild current
yellowing by the gate like home-churned butter, heard
the sound of bees humming in the bush
tiny calm midnight refrigerators
with the deep resonance of hotel pop machines.
I saw the line of blue
where sky blue met lake blue
and I dove in breathing with open eyes
and the water froze above me
like a page
made of glass.

Darling, Where Were You Besides Here?

When you feel the human heat
of sitting close in a car
and the mild narcotic of the road
miles you into sleep
and your head rolls against a shoulder
and the light fills up your little space
briefly, then goes out, lonely
like lampfire in the wind
and you dream of breathing
while the radio Beatles you
back and forth in time
so you can't believe
how your father finds his way
without maps
through the three tricky turns he must take
coming home from your grandmother's house
and you wake to the feel
of the night
in the arms of your wife
who strokes your head
and says,
"Darling, where were you
besides here?"

The Wishbone Hung by the Water Heater

My sister and I
were witching our luck
taking the furcula down
from the heater
while hot water knocked unintelligible codes in the pipes
like a plumber
trapped in a joint.
We gripped the twig-boned breast of the hen
with our thumbs
wishing for futures long forgot
on winter Sundays
when the window glass shone
like a cut face of polished coal
and the whole farm
sifted with snow.

We could have wished
for Vietnam, the Beatles,
the Bay of Pigs.
We could have wished
for the cold war, the October missile crisis,
for death in Dallas,
death on the balcony of a Memphis motel,
or death in a hot hotel kitchen in California,.
We could have wanted
presidential resignations,
Woodstocks, the accidental assassination of students,
the demise of statesmen—
Stalin, Churchill, the decline of kings.
We could have closed our eyes
to burger strips
and the quick fix.

But we were wishing
in the slow pull of the dry fork
and the feel of its own desire to stay intact, entire,

as it splintered
sending its hackle
into the little stratospheres
above our hands
a tumbling bit of nothing
chiselled at our feet
both of us secretly gratified
for what the other had been denied
as we moved ahead in the existential leaps and jumps of time
the mystery of my story, the history of her story:
like the sweepings
before the airy brooms of God
making it up as he goes.